Fiv

art IDEAS

STENCIL

Edited by
Fiona Mitchell

Designed and illustrated by
Chris Dymond

Contents

Hints and Tips 2
Glitter Fish 4
Dot to Dot 6
Take Two 8
Splattering 10
Mirror Patterns 12
Spray Stencils 14
Printed Paper 16
Torn Paper 18
Scrunching 20
Underwater 22
More Ideas 24

zigzag

Hints and Tips

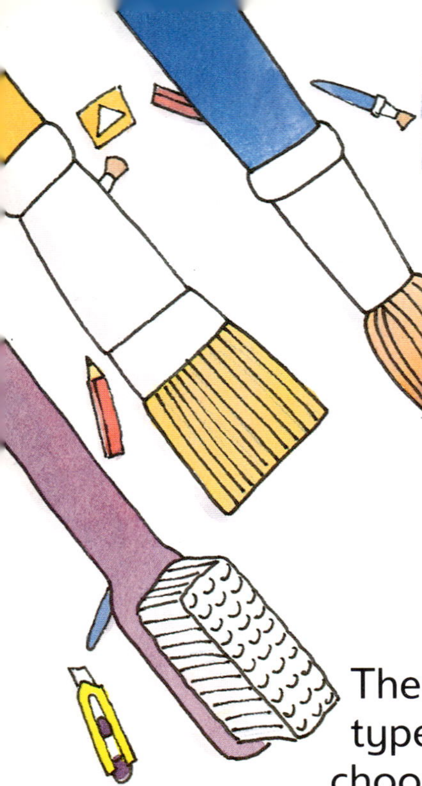

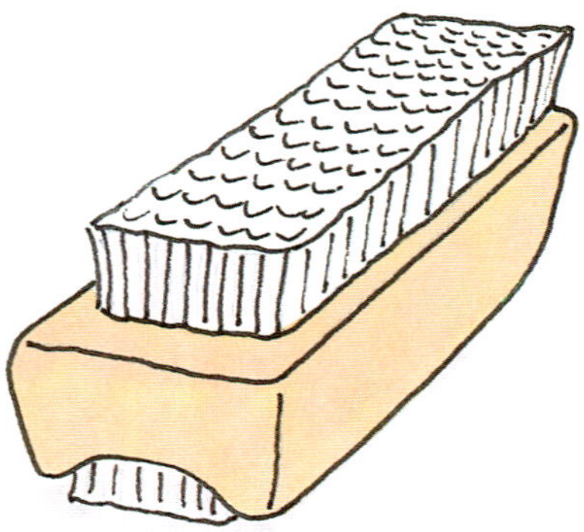

Collect together odds and ends that can be used for stencils: jam jars, leaves, string, doilies, old biros, magazines and scrap paper.

There are many different types of brushes you can choose to apply paint. Old toothbrushes and nailbrushes create an exciting effect.

Always ask an adult when you need to use a craft knife. You can buy round-ended safety scissors from most craft shops.

Instead of stencil card use cardboard from old birthday cards, cereal packets and shoe boxes.

Only use small amounts of glue to stick things together. Too much will spoil your picture.

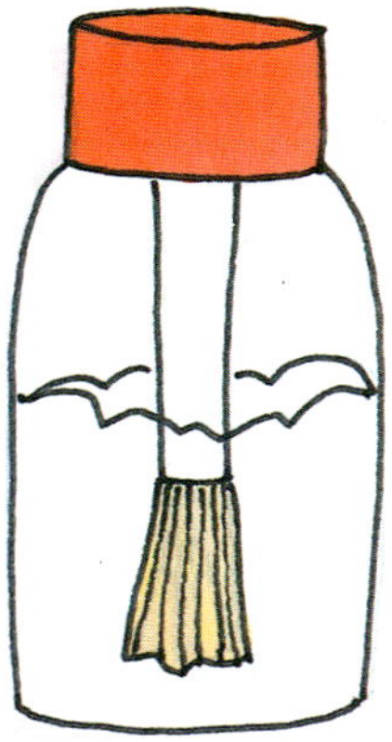

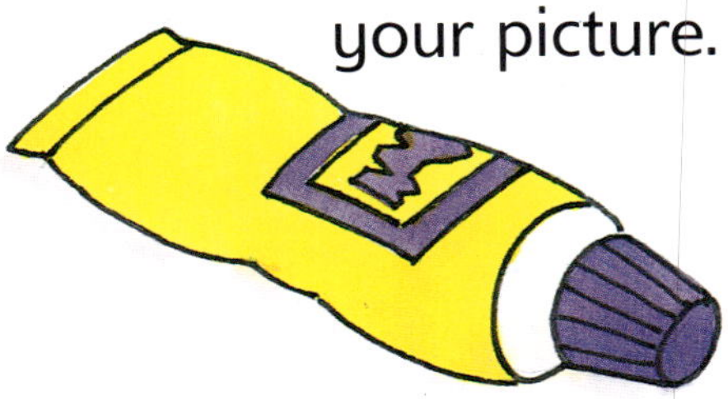

Cover your work area with plenty of newspaper. Stencilling can be very messy! Always remember to clean up afterwards.

Be imaginative! Don't just use paints for your stencil ideas. Use pens, glitter and scrunched-up tissue paper as well.

Put on an apron or old clothes before you start stencilling. This will protect your clothes from splashes of paint.

Glitter Fish

You need

1

Draw a fish in segments on the card. Carefully cut the segments out. This is your stencil.

2

Place the stencil on some thick paper. Brush the glue over the stencil.

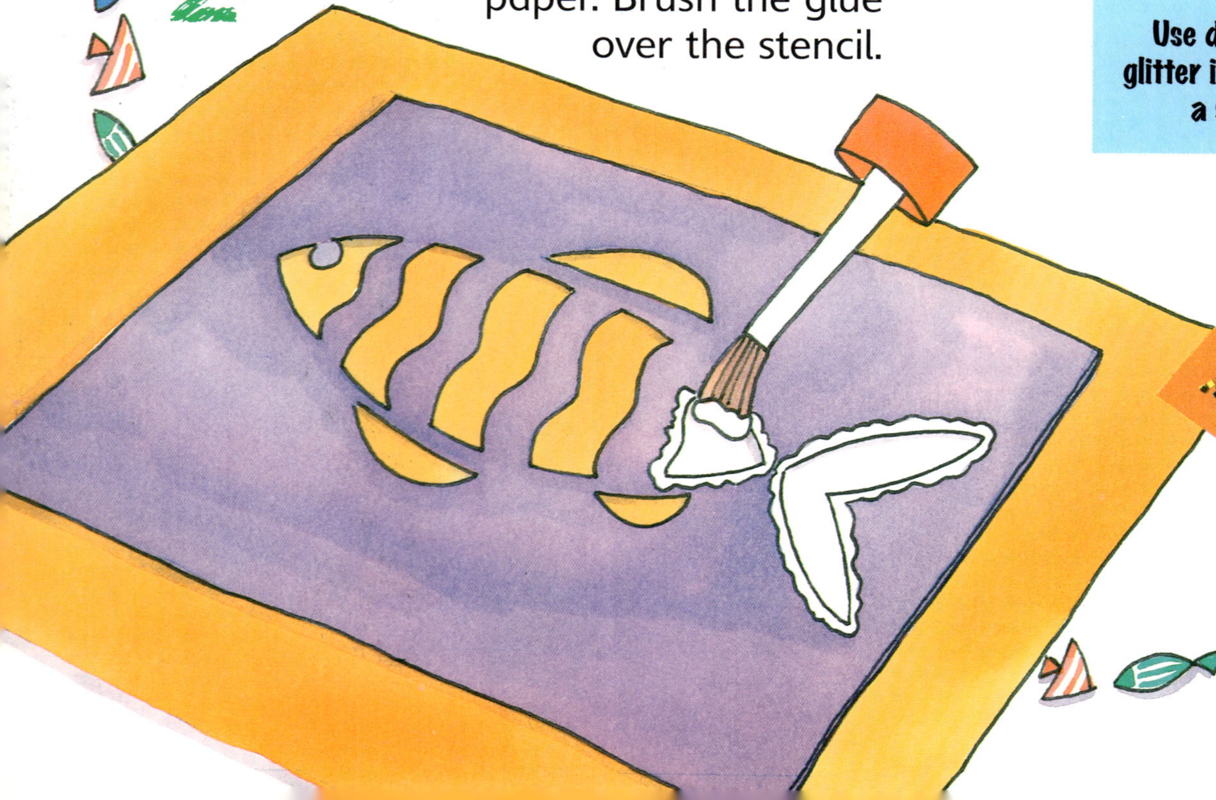

Top tip

Use different coloured glitter in each segment for a sparkling fish!

Shake the glitter over the glue and remove the stencil.

Tap off any loose glitter from your picture.

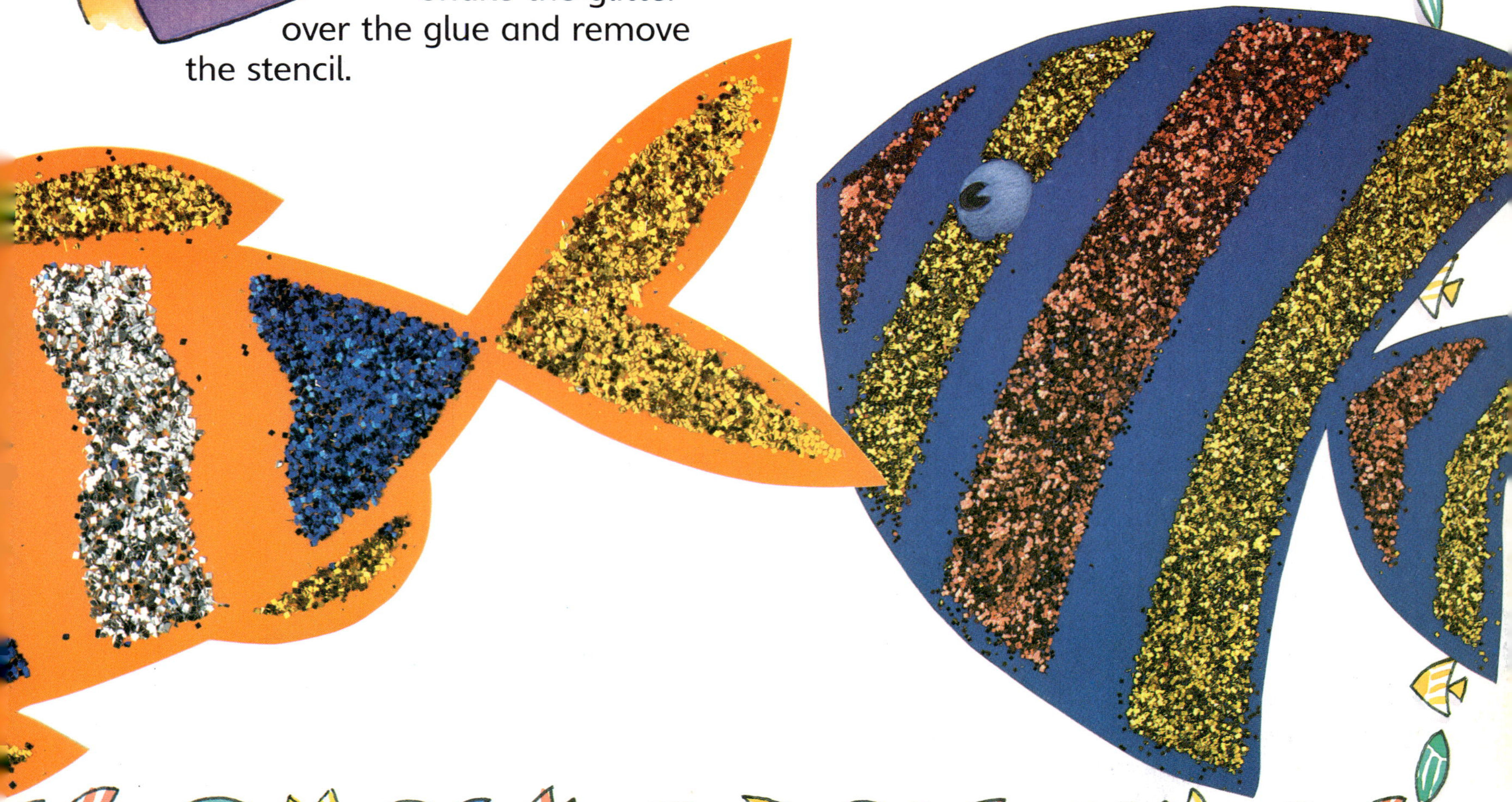

Dot to Dot

You need

1

Roll the Plasticine flat using a rolling pin. Choose a picture from an old magazine.

2

Place the picture face up over the Plasticine. Pierce holes along the lines of the picture using the nib of the old biro.

3 Turn the picture over and stick to a piece of paper using cellotape. Press the powder paint into the holes using your fingers.

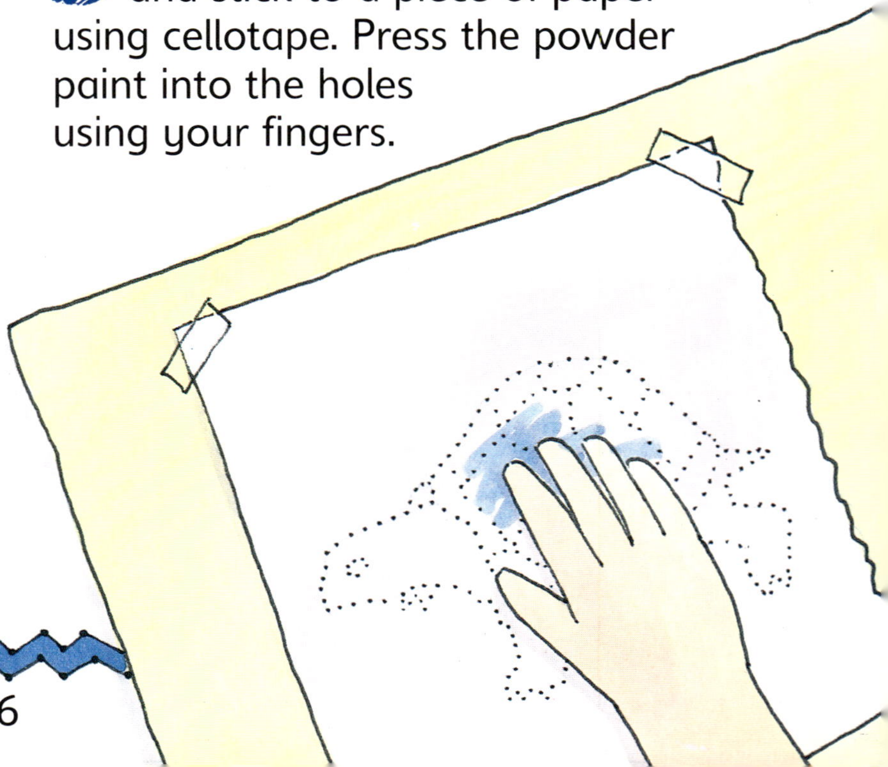

Cut out your dot to dot picture and stick it on a coloured background.

Lift the picture off the paper and you have a dotty picture! Join the dots together and colour in.

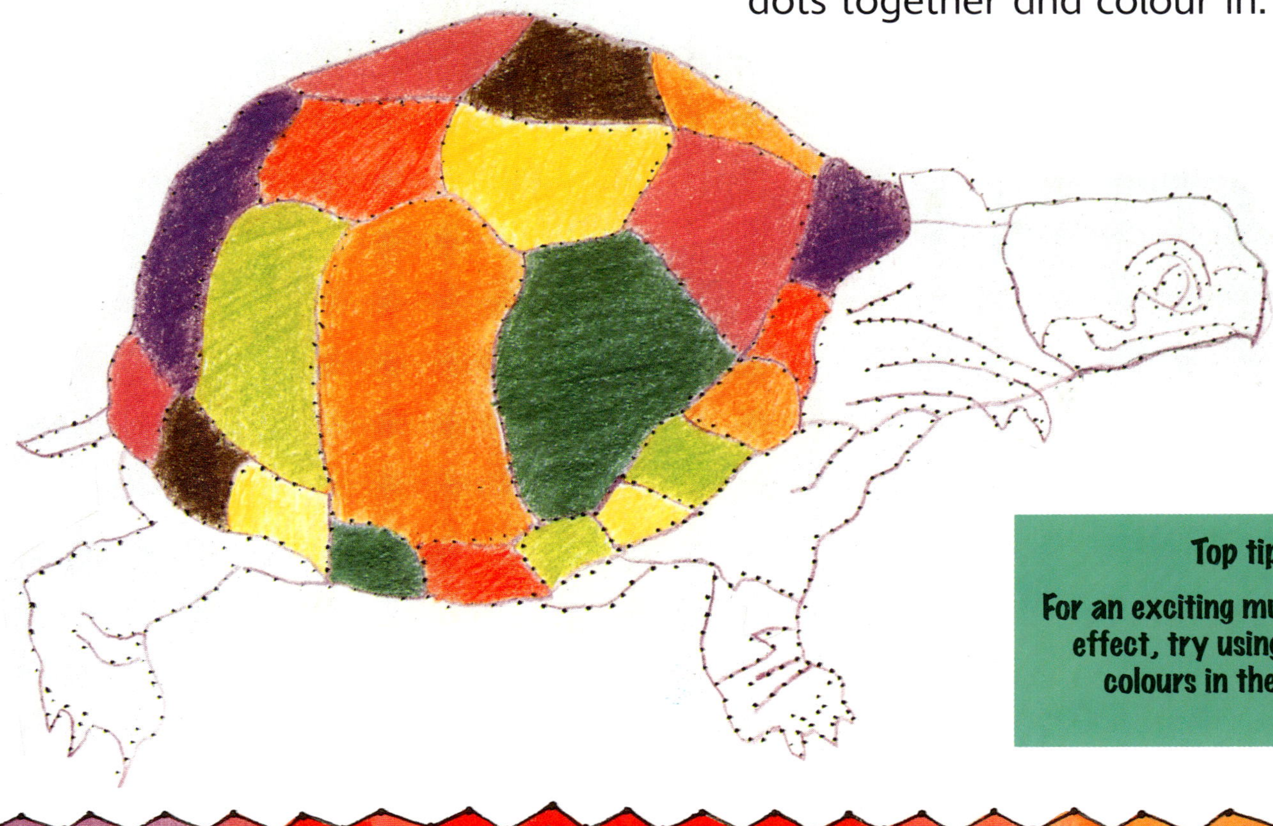

Top tip

For an exciting multi-coloured effect, try using different colours in the stencil.

Take Two

You need

Coloured paper

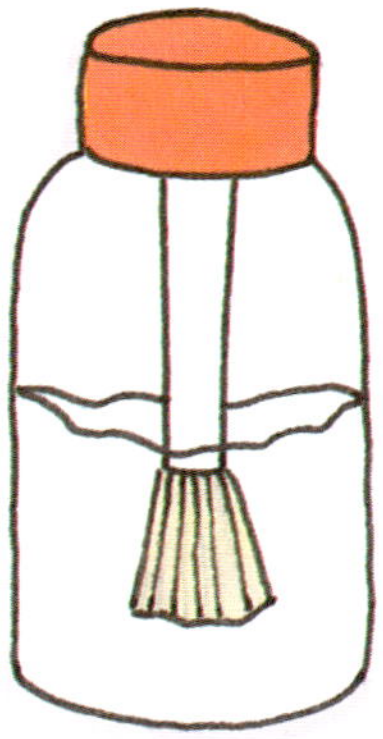
Glue

Scissors

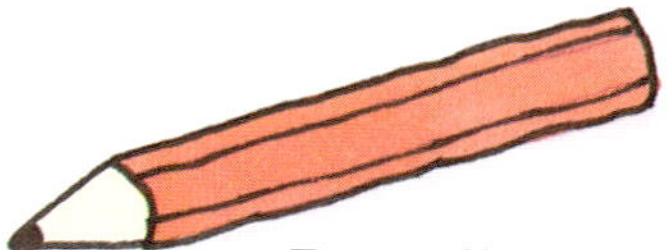
Pencil

Top tip

Make more amazing patterns by gluing lots of different stencils on top of each other.

1

Trace a round object on to paper. Cut out the circle. Fold it into four.

2

Using a pair of scissors, carefully cut shapes into the folds of the paper.

3

Unfold the paper carefully and you will have a stencil pattern. Glue it to a piece of different coloured paper to make a design.

Splattering

You need

1 Draw and cut out a picture from the card. Place the card on top of the paper.

2

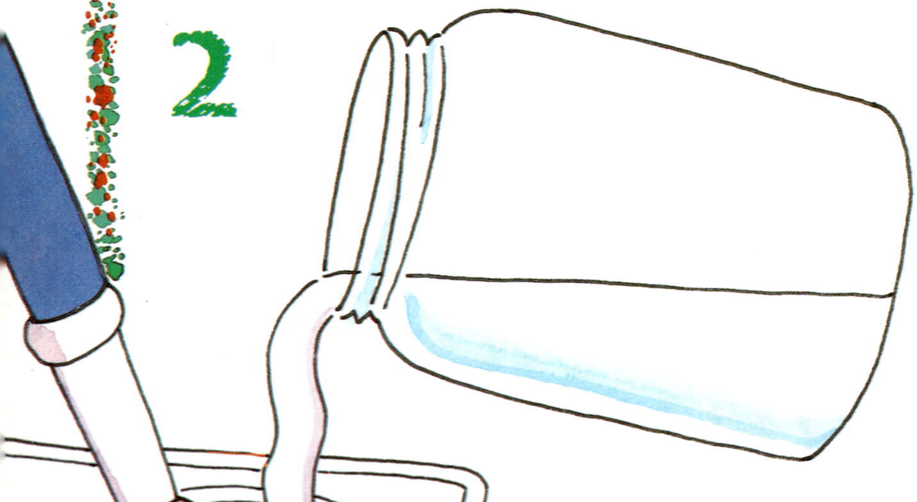

Mix up the powder paints, making sure that the paint is quite watery.

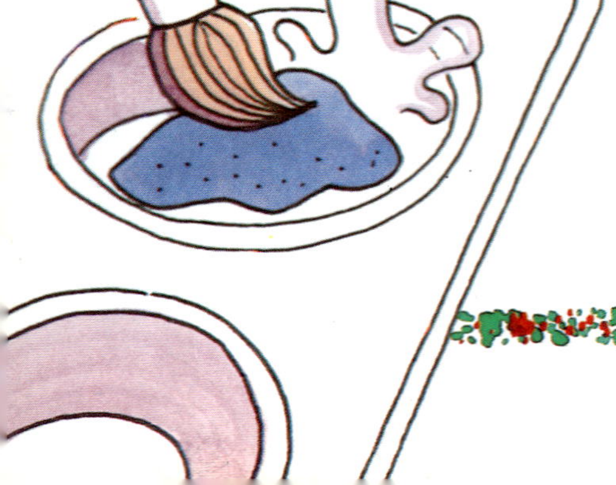

3 Dip the paintbrush into the paint and splatter paint over the stencil with a flick of the wrist.

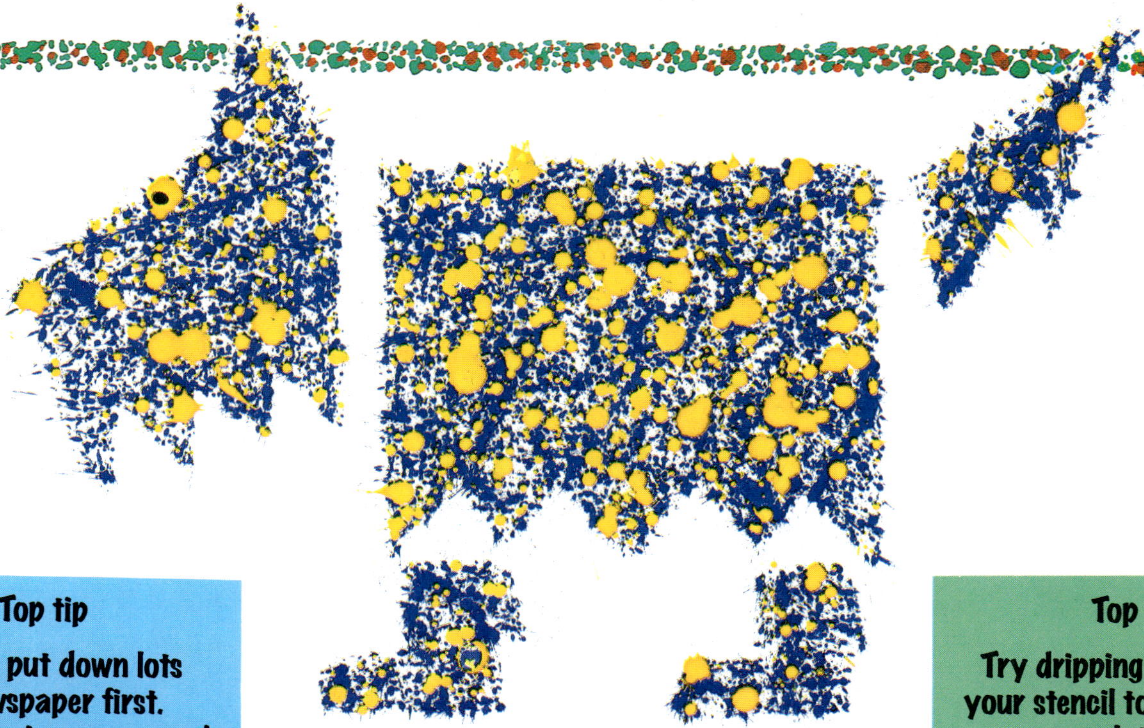

Top tip

Always put down lots of newspaper first. Splattering is very messy!

Top tip

Try dripping paint on to your stencil to get a bigger splatter.

4 Carefully remove your stencil to reveal your splatter picture.

Mirror Patterns

You need

1

Take a piece of patterned paper. Fold it in half.

2

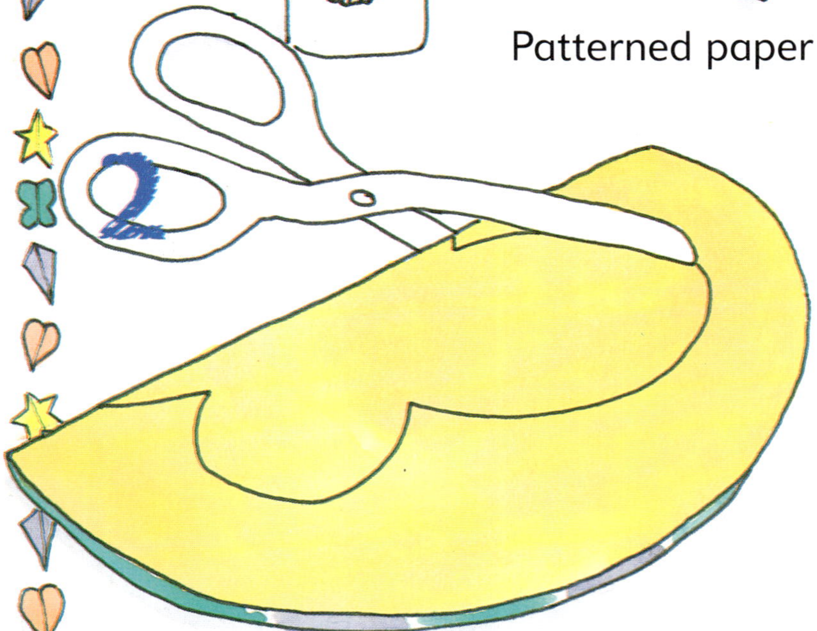

Draw half a picture from the fold in the paper. Keeping the paper folded, cut out the picture.

3

Unfold the patterned paper. You now have two stencils.

Top tip

Glue the stencils on to coloured paper to make interesting designs.

Spray Stencils

You need

1 Cut an animal shape from card using a pair of scissors. Lay the animal shape on a sheet of white paper.

2 Mix the paint with water and add a little washing-up liquid. Put the mixture into a plastic sprayer.

3 Shake the bottle well and spray the paint mixture over the stencil. Wait for the stencil to dry before you remove it.

Top tip
Be careful not to overload your toothbrush with paint or it will drip on to your stencil.

Cut a picture from card using a craft knife. Dip the toothbrush into the paint and flick the paint over the stencil.

Use as many pieces of card as you want to make the animal.

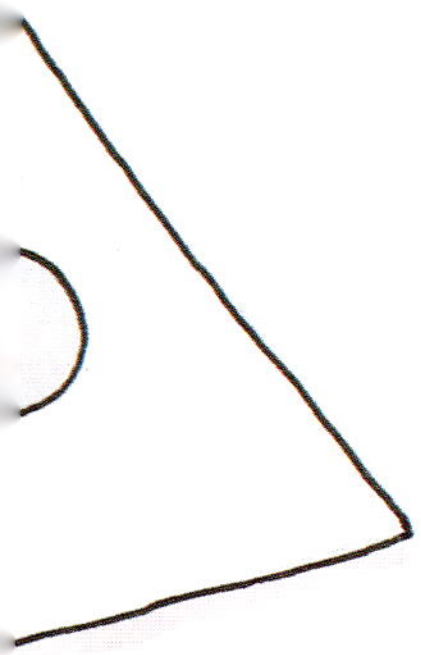

Printed Paper

You need

1

Draw some shapes on to a piece of card. Ask an adult to cut them out. This is your stencil.

2

Hold the stencil down firmly and dab the paint over it. To make a letterhead design repeat a pattern along the top of a piece of paper.

Top tip

Stencil envelopes to match your writing paper.

Dab paint on some string to match your wrapping paper.

3 To make wrapping paper, cover a large sheet of paper with a repeating pattern.

Torn Paper

You need

Paint

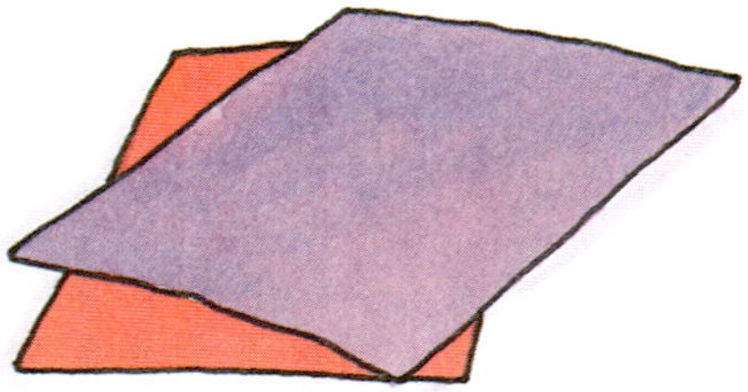

Paper

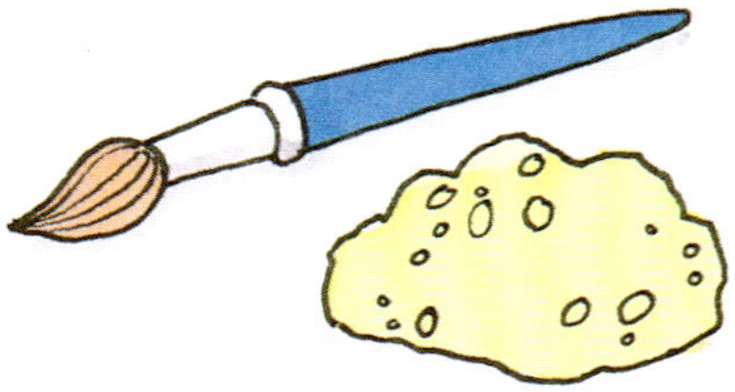

Brush or sponge

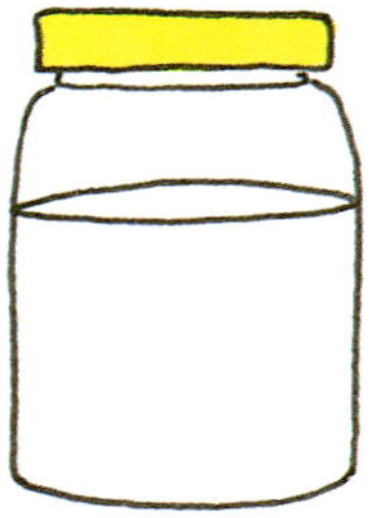

Water

1

Tear a piece of paper in half to make a zigzag shape.

2

Lay one half of the torn paper on top of a piece of coloured paper.

Try using your torn paper to make a picture.

Dab a sponge or paintbrush in some paint. Starting behind the torn edge, smear outwards.

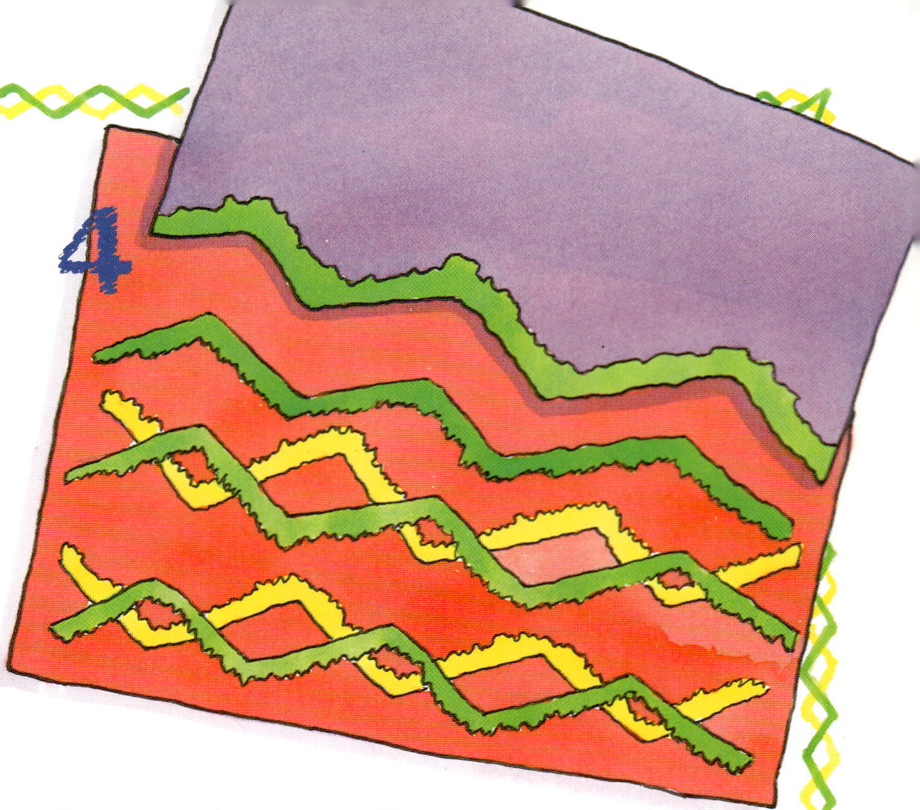

Repeat this on different parts of the paper to make a pattern.

Top tip

Try changing colours. Smear a lighter colour first, then smear a darker colour with shorter sweeps for a good effect.

Scrunching

You need

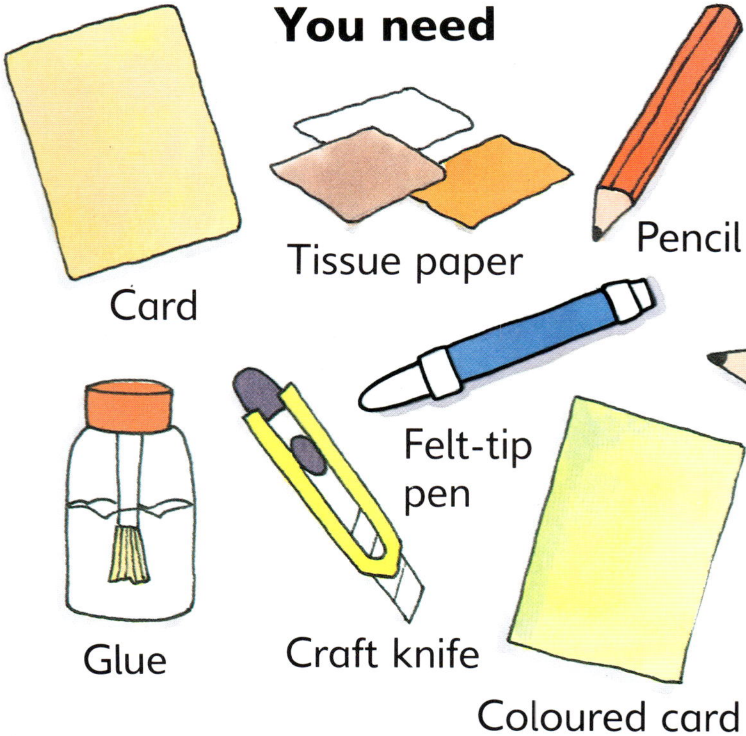

Using a pencil, draw an animal shape on to the stencil card. Ask an adult to cut the shape out using the craft knife.

Lay the animal stencil on top of a piece of coloured card. Draw around the shape using a felt-tip pen.

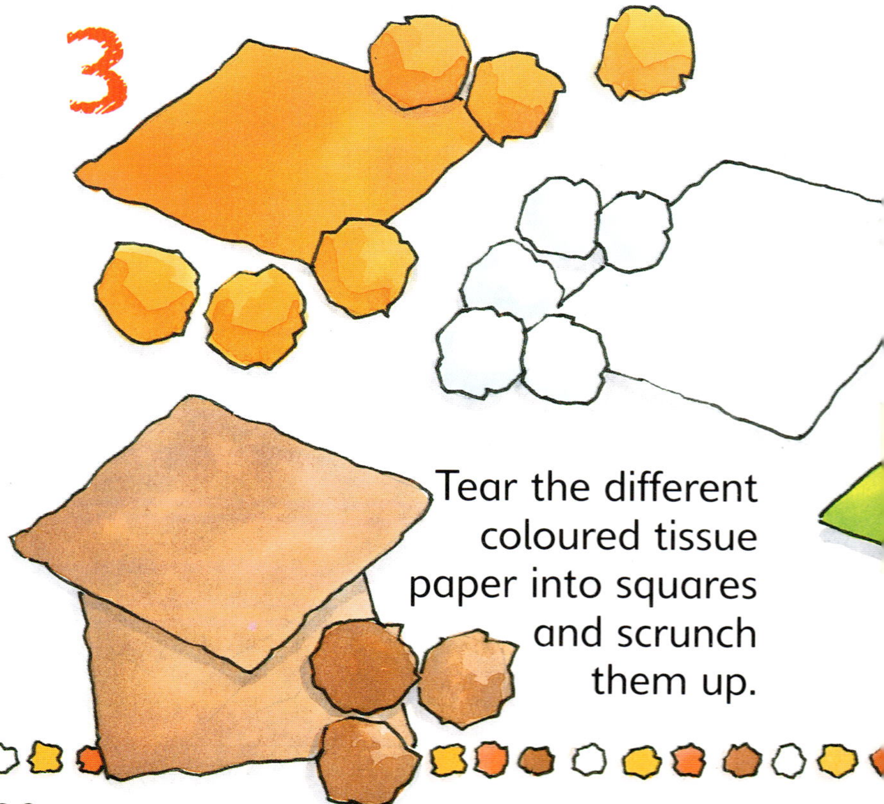

Tear the different coloured tissue paper into squares and scrunch them up.

Top tip

Put your animal in some grass. Cut a jagged edge out of green card and stick on to the bottom of your picture.

4

Glue the coloured tissue paper inside the animal shape.

Underwater

You need

1 Draw some underwater creatures and plants on to a piece of card.

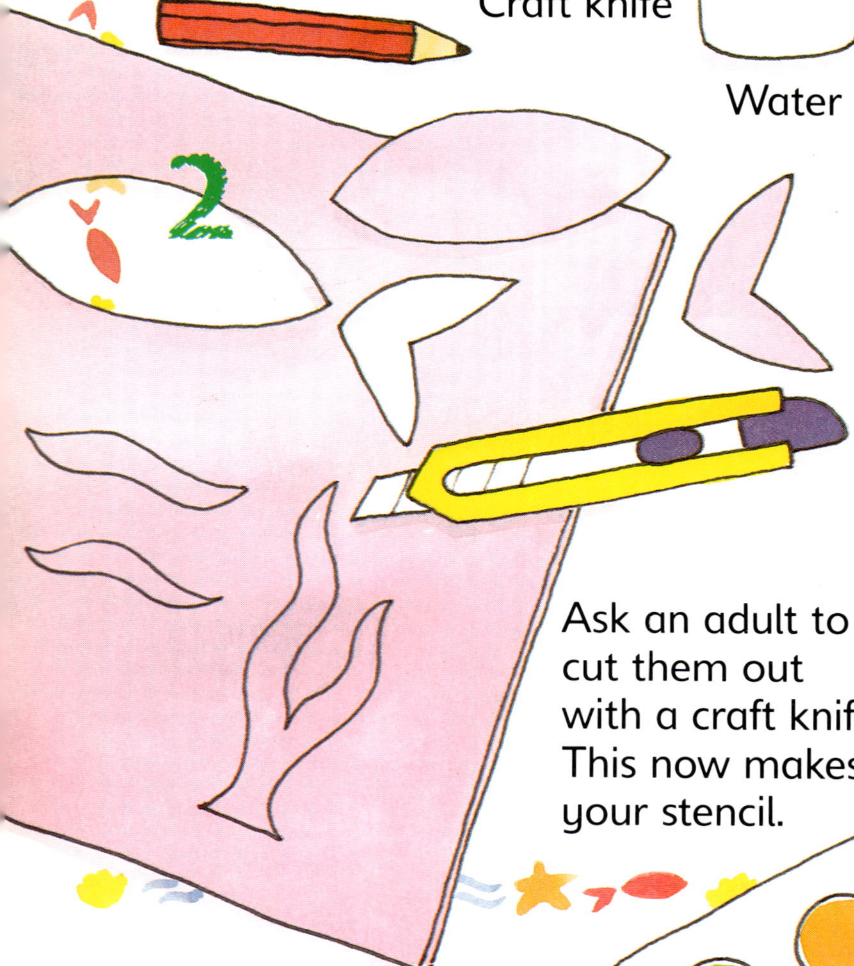

2 Ask an adult to cut them out with a craft knife. This now makes your stencil.

3 Dip the brush into the paint. Press the stencil firmly down on to a sheet of paper and dab the brush on top of it.